A Praying Mother

Frances Lang

PUBLISHED by PARABLES
Earthly Stories with a Heavenly Meaning

A Praying Mother
Frances Lang

Published By Parables
November, 2020

All Rights Reserved. No part of this book may be reproduced or utilized in any form or by any means, electronic or mechanical, including photocopying, recording, or by any information storage and retrieval system, without permission in writing from the author.

ISBN 978-1-951497-96-5
Printed in the United States of America

Readers should be aware that Internet Web sites offered as citations and/or sources for further information may have been changed or disappeared between the time this was written and the time it is read.

A Praying Mother

Frances Lang

PUBLISHED by PARABLES
Earthly Stones with a Heavenly Meaning

Chapter 1

I can remember back to about 5 years of age. My mom and dad were together. Although I had both parents, my dad (Chester) had the greater impact on my siblings and I. Chester was a spiritual man. He made it a point to take his children to Church. Not only did we attend service, we were also involved with services by taking roles for Christmas celebrations and Easter plays. We were always well dressed on Sundays. One of my favorite memories was Easter. My sister Tudy and I were the youngest girls so naturally we were spoiled. On this particular Easter Sunday, the girls had skirt suits with fishnet stockings, white gloves, white patent leather shoes and purses. My brothers Darryl, Wesley and Warren, were dressed in nice slacks, ties, and topped off with trench coats. Like most days but especially this day, we were proud to be the Roland family.

Chester was not only spiritual man, but he was a man who liked things to be nice and clean, decent and in order. Every Saturday he made us thoroughly clean the house. We would clean cabinets, mop and dust. My dad would even put on a white glove to examine the dusting. The things that he instilled in me, even at such young age, stuck with me. There were two things my dad ask of me. He said "baby girl, I encourage you to 1. Go to Church and 2. Get your education." I was about 7 years old when my dad said that to me.

My dad eventually split from my mother and moved to Emporia, KS. He had only been there a very short time before

things started changing. My mom received a phone call to come to visit him because he had been sick. Mom had taken all of us children to our grandmothers house (her mom) until she returned. When mom arrived in Emporia she was presented with some very bad news. Unfortunately, my dad had died. The cause of death was a brain hemorrhage. He was only 38 years of age. Mom came in the house and sat us down to tell us what she learned in Emporia. She said in a soft shaking voice,
"Your dad died this morning".
We all started crying. We were shocked because dad was so young. Thanksgiving was only four days away. It was a sad one without my dad but we still had a lot to be thankful to the Lord for.

    Things eventually changed in our home. Mom didn't take us to Church. She barely made us clean up. There was very little guidance for us. Nevertheless, I would spend the weekends, with Dear (paternal grandmother). Dear had eight children: Dewitt, Chester, Phillip, Carl Eugene Sr., Frances Marie, Martha, and Judith Carol. Dear and Grandpa Roland raised them all in Church. They all are successful Christians.

    Dear would teach me about the Lord. "Don't be cutting up or the Lord can't bless you." She would say to me. That statement stuck with me all my life. I never wanted the Lord to stop blessing me. In any situation, I tried to do what was right to do.

    There was a custody battle sometime after dad died. Dear had the desire to have custody of my dad's children. My mom had 2 other girls from previous relationships. I was anticipating living with Dear because I fell in love with Jesus at an early age. I also love to go to Church. When Dear and mom went to court my mom won the custody battle. I was disappointed that Dear lost to mom, but I thanked the Lord our bond was never broken.

A Praying Mother

When mom won custody of her children, she was awarded a lot of money. To celebrate her victory, she decided to take us on a trip. We all chose to go to six flags in St. Louis Mo. She took us all shopping for new clothes and she took us girls to her beautician (Gaitan) to get our hair done. We were so excited about the trip. Mom and her boyfriend drove her car. She had a green Electric 225. When we arrived in St. Louis, we checked into our hotels. The girls had a room and the boys had a room. We went swimming and everything. Before we knew it, it was time to get dressed to go to six flags. We could hardly wait to get to six flags. When we arrived at six flags, as soon as mom parked, we jumped out of the car to run for the train. My family had our focus on riding all the rides in the park that were on our level. We had a joyous time at six flags. Mom let us stay until it closed. We were so tired and ready to go to bed. The next morning we went to the St. Louis Arch. The arch was interesting, but not as fun as six flags. After the third day we headed back home. We saw some nice sights. We had lots of fun on our trip. I am reminded how well my brother and sisters and I got along. We had lots of fun together all the time, except for our oldest sister Tamia. Tamia had issues she use to whip me for no reason at all, or should I say no good reason. I use to tell my mom but she never did anything about it. I wanted to run away from home because things had gotten so bad in my teenage years.

Meanwhile back at the house (I called it the land of do what you wanna do), Mom was still the same. She would go to bingo and work a job. I was growing up and starting to face challenges, especially with boys. I had to do the right thing like my grandmother had taught me. My mom was doing the best she could with life. She was basically making choices and decisions that she knew to do according to her knowledge. What made the difference between Mom and Dear was, Dear was teaching us to live by the bible and God's Commandments. Mom had no real standards for us to live by.

We had next door neighbor named Mrs. Polly. She called a meeting for all the children in the neighborhood. We met on her front porch. The meeting was about having bible study. She wanted us to have bible study every Wednesday afternoon. All the children agreed. When Wednesday came, we were all sitting on her front porch on time for bible class. Mrs. Polly not only taught us from the bible, but she taught us Church songs. After lessons we would have a drink and a snack. She had two daughters, Verde and Sandra, they would help her serve us.
Mrs. Polly was blessed. She had observed and she knew that none of the parents were taking their children to church. To make up for the lack in morals, she found a way to teach us about the love of Jesus Christ and how to start living for Him, and show Him that we love Him too. Mrs.
Polly said "Jesus is coming back again! I hope you all be ready." I learned a lot from Mrs. Polly. She kept me right on track from what my dad and Dear were teaching me.

My mom was dating a guy named Jamal. It was rumor that he was doing drugs. I knew he smoked weed. One day my brothers, sisters and I were eating dinner when all of a sudden the police kicked our door in. They came in the dining room where we were eating. They start pouring out our juice and looking through our food. We were wondering what was going on! They went through the house tearing up everything. Mom was not home.
The police didn't stop until they ransacked the entire house. They didn't find any drugs. They left promising that they would come back if another call was made. When we told my mom what happened she was mad at the police. She said that Jamal didn't

really live with us he just stay over sometimes, and that he would never bring drugs to our house because of us. Again, this is the land of do what you want to do.

Frances Lang

Chapter 2

As I was growing up, I became interested in dancing. I would dance around at home. Mom noticed my interest and enrolled me into a professional dance class. I studied modern jazz, tap, and light ballet. I took classes at the Turner House. My dance instructor's name was Connie. Connie chose me out of the whole class to do a ballet solo. The challenge was that I had to perform in her studio in Missouri. I had to learn the dance piece in one evening. I was like wow! She had confidence in me. She told me she knew I could do it and that's why she chose me. She said I dance great and I catch on fast. My mom took me to her dance studio in Mo. I learned the dance piece in one evening just like Connie requested. I performed in a recital the next day. I performed to the song Climb Every Mountain. I wore a white sequence blouse with a full round length sequence skirt, white leotard, and white ballet shoes. When it was time for me to perform I was confident in what Connie had taught me. After my performance, I was walking off stage and suddenly I was surprised, Connie had grabbed me, hugged me real tight and told me how proud she was of me. I felt glad that I took the challenge. I also took classes at the Academy of

Performing Arts. I love to dance. It's so much fun. I made up this robot dance that everyone loved. Children would pay me 25 cents to do the robot. I was recognized by Bobby a member of the Junior Lockers. This was a group of dancers that was similar to the real Lockers that you saw on TV (soul train). Bobby asked me did I want to dance in his group. He said I could be their robot for the junior Lockers since the real Lockers had a robot dancer. Of course, my answer was yes.

I felt like it was an honor. After all, I was the only girl dancing with the Junior Lockers. We danced outside around the playground in front of our apartments. I enjoyed rehearsals because not only were they making me their robot dancer, but they were teaching me to dance like the Lockers.

Bobby's Mom asked me if I would like to go to Church with them. I said yes.

The name of the church is Pleasant Green Baptist Church. They started a van service for the

children that lived in our apartments. Now I could attend Church on a regular basis. By this time, I was in Junior High School. I was on the Honor Society throughout all of Junior High School.

I attended Northeast Jr. High School. I had a favorite teacher. Her name is Mrs. Norwood. She would tell me how to have confidence in myself. The things a mother would tell her daughter. She taught Spanish. I was in her class for two years. I excelled in her class and she was so proud of me. One thing that made her upset is her class saying the Spanish alphabet too slow. She would find out what class I was in and have me report to her class immediately. When I arrived, she would be waiting for me with a pointer in her hand. She asked me to show her class how they are to recite the alphabet in Spanish. She would start hitting that pointer on the chalk board. I would start reciting the Spanish alphabet as fast as she could hit that pointer. The class would be in awe. Mrs. Norwood would then thank me and send me back to my class. Mrs. Norwood did this on several occasions. I didn't really think much of it but I had learned to recite the Spanish alphabet as fast as I could recite the English alphabet, if not faster. Mrs. Norwood was like a second mother to me. She would leave the school sometimes to take care of her business and she would take me with her.

While attending Northeast, I participated in the talent shows that they present every year. The best talent show I remember was the one held my freshman year. I started a new group called the Lockerettes. I chose 3 other girls to dance with me. I had to teach them some of the Locker moves that I had learned from the Jr. Lockers. Brenda Reliford, my best friend, could robot already. She and I had also learned some mime. We did a lot of rehearsing to prepare for the talent show. I asked permission for the Junior Lockers to perform in the talent show.

The Lockerettes performed to the song "Get the funk out of my face" by Brother Johnsons. The talent show was awesome! The Junior Lockers performed to the song "Dancing Machine" by The Jacksons. The Junior Lockers showed out! The Lockerettes were good too. Everyone enjoyed the talent show. Teachers, students, and parents were talking about the talent show for months.

I joined the choir at Northeast. It was directed by Mrs. Barnes. I enjoyed singing with the choir. Later, I joined the Church Choir at Guiding Star Missionary Baptist Church and Pleasant Green Baptist Church. No matter what choices I made in my life, I was determined to keep Jesus first. I have a lot of great memories of my adventures at Northeast Jr. High School.

Frances Lang

Chapter 3.

I was attending Washington High my sophomore year. Unfortunately, there was a lot of fighting and discrimination transpiring at school. For these reasons, I didn't like school. The series "Roots" was being shown on TV at this time which caused most of the racial tension.
Students were segregating at an intergraded school. The students had a hallway for the African Americans, and a hallway for the Whites. You could only walk down the hallway of your color or you would be beat up. Some of the teachers were prejudice too.

My junior year was better. The racial differences were not as prominent. This was the time that boys really started to notice me

When I became a senior, I had achieved honor roll grades. The Lord blessed me with a part-time job working at Wendy's restaurant. I worked after school and on the weekends. I had enough money to buy my own school clothes and everything. I met this college student from Ottawa University his name is Renny. He liked me. He wanted me to be his girlfriend. We dated. We attended a revival. He would come over to my house. While Renny was "dating me Victor was pursuing me. Victor was coming to my job flirting with me. He was coming on strong. One of his pickup lines was "Can I have her with everything on her to go." He was winking at me. I was trying so hard to ignore him but he was an attractive guy.

One day Renny and Victor came up to my job, almost at the same time. First Victor came up to me at the counter and said "I'm here to pick you up". Renny comes up to the counter shortly after and said the same thing. I ran to the back room to try and decide which one of them I wanted to leave with. My co-workers were laughing at me and teasing me. I said I was trying to ignore Victor be really deep down inside I was attracted to him. I had been skating with him and he had a talent for skating that I admired. Not only did I like Victor, but I'd been hearing rumors that Renny was a player. I came to the conclusion that I was going to leave with Victor. That's what I did. I left Renny sitting in the dining room.

    Victor asked me out on a date. The date was going to a haunted house. I didn't like that but Victor talked me into going he said "I'll be holding you real tight". Victor actually held me tight. After our date was over, we decided to keep on dating. For our second date, and I met at Washington's homecoming game. We left the game a little early because we desired to be alone. The next date Victor ask me if I would come to Church with him. One thing led to another, and it was time to meet his parents. When I saw his mother I thought she was white, but she is Irish and his dad is African American. After I met his parents, Victor and I were asked to meet over his brother, Thomas, house. However when we arrived, his brother explained to Victor that his mom and dad were afraid of our relationship. Victor assured him that he loved me and there was no reason for them to be afraid.

    I love Christmas and sure enough it was the Christmas Season! Victor came to my house with 5 big boxes. I stood in the door watching him bring the boxes in. I couldn't help but wonder what he had bought me. My family was shocked! When I opened the boxes clothes were in them. I had sweaters with matching pants.

    Victor and I continued to date. We went to the movies, we did a lot of skating and we spent time at his house and at mine. One day we were together at my house and I fell asleep on

Victor's lap. While sleeping, I felt tears dropping on my face. Victor was crying. I raised up to comfort him. Victor said "I'm going to get you out of this house", then he left for the evening. I knew what he was talking about. My mom's house wasn't clean. I was uncomfortable with some of my siblings as well. Especially Tamia. Tamia didn't like Victor. Victor and I were in the living room kissing. She saw us and told us to get out.

    I never understood what her problem was. It was close to Graduation day and, Tamia approached me threatening to whip me. Again, I hadn't done anything wrong. I stood up to her. I said "you are not going to touch me, those days are over! I'm graduating from school." I quickly got out of the door and went to my friend Sissy's house.

Sissy's mom was having my graduation gown cleaned. I told Sissy what was going on at my house. Sissy told me she had seen Tamia drunk one time. I realized when she was talking to me she couldn't have been in her right mind. Fortunately, I never had a problem with her putting her hands on me again. Although she did talk crazy sometime.

    At graduation time Victor and I were still in a close relationship with each other and becoming more serious about our relationship. I invited him to my graduation. Victor seemed to be the right guy for me. He was spending lots of time and money on me. He was showing me that he had love for me. He even cared about my situation at home.

    Graduation May of 1980, was held at Washington High School. My Mom and Mrs. Taylor attended my graduation, and of course Victor was there. I graduated in the upper-third of my class. During the ceremony, when they called out my name, I could hear Victor shouting out my name. I knew he was proud of me. My mom and my family were proud of me.

The Taylor's were happy for me as well. When the graduation was over, Victor was waiting for me outside. He said "let's go celebrate", so we left.

During our celebration, Victor took me to a friend's house who apparently was not at home. He convinced me to drink. I had never drank before. However, I had gotten drunk and one thing led to another.. The next day Victor told me that I was pregnant. I didn't believe him at first. As the months went by I started having symptoms. First, there was morning sickness, then my figure began to change. By the time I went to see the doctor I was already 3 months pregnant.

Victor was attending (BRAC) Brotherhood of Railway and Airline Clerks. He was at the top of his class and next in line for a job. Thanks to the Lord, Victor was chosen for the job opening at the Santa Fe Railroad in Topeka, KS. His position was in the office as a clerk. Victor gave me the good news about his new job. He also proposed to me. I said yes. My life began to change.

Mrs. Taylor helped me to move in their house. The plan was for me to live with his parents until our child was born. Mrs. Taylor bought me maternity clothes and talk to me about the Lord. Victor came home every weekend to spend time with me and his family as we waited for our wedding day

Chapter 4

December 13, 1980 Victor and I were married at Guiding Star Missionary Baptist Church with the blessing of Reverend Rice. The wedding was small but it was formal. However, I was running late for my wedding. They tell me Victor was having a fit. He was hoping that I would not leave him at the Altar. I showed up late, wearing a Royal blue wedding gown. Victor had on a suit. The ceremony went on. My step dad gave me away.

Shortly after we were married, LaTosha was born. February 15, 1981. LaTosha and I continued to live with Victor's parents. In the meantime, Victor had acquired about a place for us in Topeka. I didn't know for sure if our living situation had changed. Victor picked me up to go to our apartment in Topeka one day. He asked me to stay in the car. When he got back in the car he said he had to make a stop. We pulled up to this pretty house. He ask me to get out of the car and go to the door with him. He opened the door with the key he had and "Surprise!" He said. There on the wall was a big banner that read "Welcome home Frances and LaTosha, hugs and kisses. I love you". I was surprised. It was a big step up from the apartment we had.

Although Victor had acquired a house for us we still did not move in with him. I had decided to attend (BRAC) and prepare myself for a job working for Santa Fe Railroad with Victor. LaTosha stayed home with her grandmother while I was attending BRAC training. I spent time in Topeka with my spouse on the weekends.

Every time I went to Topeka I found out something different about Victor. He was exploring different things at this point of his life. We were invited to a gathering over one of his friend's house. The gathering consist of doing drugs, and watching porn movies. I just sat there quietly and watched. I was ready to go as soon as we got there. Later on, when Victor and I arrived at home, he got angry with me. He said "I'm sick of you being Ms. Goody two shoes and ruining all the fun for everyone". I stood up to him and said "I didn't do drugs before I met you and I'm not going to do drugs now!" Victor grabbed me and tried to make me sniff some drug that he had. I fought and broke away from him. I knew then that the new job and all the money was changing him. He was trying to change me too.

When I arrived in KC I was glad to be away from Victor. It was on a Sunday morning.
Instead of going to his parents Church, I went to my Church and talked to my pastor, Rev. Rice.
I had a chance to speak with him. I asked him "can you marry someone that God didn't intend for you to marry"? He replied," Yes, when you go home God will show you." Therefore I went home to pray. I prayed "Lord I know you don't like divorce but if this marriage is not in your will for me help me to end it and go on with my life." I didn't talk to his mom and dad about what was going on with him.

Now BRAC was offering me a job. I was on top of my class so the railroad was asking for me. The job offer was for the Southern Pacific in Louisiana. I did not accept the job offer. God had not answered my prayer yet concerning my marriage. Finally I made a trip back home after talking to Rev. Rice. When I arrived at home I was very quiet. I sat down and was looking around the house. I saw Victor's drug paraphernalia laying on the table. That made me feel so different about our relationship. I sat on a sofa he was not sitting on. We were watching Dallas on TV. JR Ewing had women all over him. Victor said "Why are you sitting over there? Why aren't you sitting by me?" Then he said "JR Ewing has all kinds of women loving on him." I said "Maybe JR Ewing is doing something right for them to love on him." Victor got mad. We started arguing. Victor left shortly after. I was asleep while he was gone. When I woke up it was dark. The Lord told me to put on my coat, it was summer, but I didn't question Him. When Victor came home he was still mad. He starting hitting me with a belt. He realized I had my coat on, he took my coat off, pushed me in the bathroom, raised the belt up in the air and said "you are going to do what I want you to do regardless of what I do!" I screamed "JESUS!" with all my might. As loud as I could. Victor immediately fell to his knees and dropped the belt. I ran out of the house and to the store. There, I used a payphone. I called his mom in KC and told her what was happening. She told me I had to wait until morning before she could pick me up. Later, Victor came looking for me on his motorcycle. He found me at the neighborhood store. He looked up at me and said "You didn't get a ride did you"? He zoomed down the street. I knew then he was still up to no good since he didn't offer me a ride home and it was dark outside. Now I was asking the Lord to lead me. I was not going back in to the house with him. Not after what I had just experienced. I walked back down the street. When I came passed the house Victor was standing in the door, trying to hide that belt behind his back. I start screaming for help. He started chasing me. All of a sudden, our neighbor opened her door and I ran inside. Victor was trying to tell our neighbor that I was his spouse and he wasn't trying to hurt me. I told the lady that I really didn't know him. In reality I did not. She closed her door. She and I talked. I told her how he was trying to beat me. She asked me did I want to stay in a battered women shelter. I said yes. Although the Lord protected me from being battered, I needed a place to be safe from Victor until morning. Therefore, my neighbor called the police and they took me to the women's shelter.

During my time at the shelter, I was learning about how men abuse and mistreat women. One lady said her spouse took her for a walk. They walked into the woods. He took off his belt, then beat her unmercifully. She said he did not even give her a reason why. He just beat her for no reason. No one could hear her scream. After hearing my story, she said she wished she would have called Jesus. Another lady said her spouse threw a fork at her and stuck her in her eye. I heard several stories that night. God answered my prayer that night. The Bible says in 1 Corinthians 7:13 "And the woman which hath a husband that believeth not, and if he be pleased to dwell with her, let her not leave him." Victor was not pleased with me trusting and living for the Lord. He tried to change me. Since he couldn't change me, he tried to beat me. I know the Lord set me free. I'm going to walk in my freedom.

Chapter 5

The next day my mom and Ms. Taylor came to Topeka to take me back to KC with them. When we arrived in KC, I asked to go to the attorney's office. I wanted to file for a divorce, and that's just what I did. We took mom home, then we arrived at Mrs. Taylor's house. We had a talk. I explained to her why I was going through with the divorce. I even told her about Victor being on drugs and the kind of friends he chose to be with. I also explained to her that I had the desire to be married to the same man for life.. My dream was crushed. I cried. Later on that day, I heard Mrs. Taylor in her bedroom crying. She cried much more than I did. She told me that day that LaTosha and I could live there with her and Mr. Taylor as long as we needed.

Nevertheless, I was waiting for the divorce to become final. Victor decided to come stay at his parent's house for the weekend. I knew that I had to leave. I went to stay at my mom's house. After all, my attorney advised me not to spend the night wherever Victor may be during the trial period. The day came for us to finally be divorced. I met my attorney at the Kansas District Courthouse. I took the stand. I actually had to explain to the Judge why I should be granted a divorce. When I looked out in the courtroom, Victor was crying like a baby. I asked the judge could I step out of the courtroom. He granted my request. My attorney and I stepped out into the hallway. I said to my attorney "After all he's been doing I can't believe he is in there crying." It was a brief chat. The Judge was calling us right back into the courtroom. The Judge had granted the divorce. He asked me if I wanted alimony, the house, or the car. I didn't want anything but he insist

I take child support. The divorce was granted July 7, 1983. I was awarded full custody of LaTosha and child support was mandatory.

Chapter 6

    Life being a single mother wasn't so easy at first. I had to learn how to be independent and stand on my own. I had not acquired my independence as of yet. While I was working toward stability, I felt like it was in the best interest of LaTosha and I to continue to live with her grandparents.

    I completed BRAC training. The Lord bless me with a job at the Wyandotte County Health Department as a clerk. While I was working at the health department, Mrs. Taylor came up with a plan for me to sign guardianship papers for LaTosha in event of an emergency. I felt like I had no other choice but to sign the guardianship papers since I was living in their house. Therefore, I signed the guardianship papers. I started feeling the pressure of not having my own place or having some relative that I could live with. Victor was not helping. He would not pay his child support. I just wanted to be free from the Taylors. All this stress led up to me being hospitalized for a few days. I had to keep my faith in God even though I saw no way out of the situation. During the short time I was hospitalized, Victor and his parents had a judge to give him custody of LaTosha. Isaiah 54:17 No weapon formed against me shall prosper.

Frances Lang

Chapter 7

The first thing I did to regain custody of LaTosha was called my attorney that represented me at the time of the divorce. He was able to move the court to grant me a petition. The court petition stated that the petitioner must provide a place of residence of her own to accommodate her and the minor child. She shall then have custody of the minor child.

I began dating a young man by the name of Franklin I met him while I was at the bus stop one day. He began to really get serious about me. He eventually proposed to me. We became engaged. When he told his Mother she was against our relationship. She and Mrs. Taylor were good friends. They lived around the corner from each other. Franklin began to become confused about me because of the lies they were telling about me. I started referring to him as momma's boy. I told him that I did not want to be engaged to him anymore. Because, He didn't have a mind of his own. We broke up. Shortly after we broke up. I found out I was pregnant. There was no way I was giving this child up, or risking another custody battle with a marriage to a man that didn't really have agape love for me.

I talked to my Uncle Corky. I explained to him the fulfillment of the petition and that I needed a place to live until I establish a place of my own. He welcomed me to come live with him and his family at his house. I lived with my Uncle Corky and my Aunt Norma until I established an apartment of my own. Of course my life was still going on, so by the time I fulfilled the court order I had given birth to another child. My son Isaiah.

I had my attorney to petition the court to grant me the custody of LaTosha according to the allegations stated in the petition. I had acquired an apartment that was safe, secure and healthy environment. For some reason those judges in division 6 did not grant me the custody of LaTosha. They didn't give me a reason why they were not abiding by the petition that they wrote. It was wrong and unlawful. Once again they violated my right to a fair hearing.
I began to recall the Taylor's telling me that Thomas Taylor, Victor's brother, was one of the United States most famous men. He was also the Director of Public Affairs for
'KMBZ radio station. Victor had warned me in argument one time that if I thought I was going to live without him, that his family would have the judge to take LaTosha from me. I thought he was just talking out of anger but he really knew something. Nevertheless, I trust God and His
Word. Romans 8:31 What shall we say to these things? If God be for us who can be against us?

During this time I was seeking help. I cried day and night because they wouldn't let me see LaTosha or talk to her on the phone. They wouldn't even let me see her on Christmas Day. My heart was broken. I just continued to trust Jesus to restore me. Psalm 121 I look to the hills from whence cometh my help, my help cometh from the Lord that made Heaven and Earth.
I went to the Clerk of the District Court to see what they were displaying as the last status of the case. Judges started approaching the desk and looking at me mean. They refused to let me see my file. This was another violation of my rights. Court records are open to the public.

I ran to my attorney's office. I explained to him what was transpiring since we received the petition. He replied "I can no longer represent you." I knew then that there was a conspiracy in progress. However, I still asked the attorney for my file. When I had the file in my hand his phone rang. The Lord told me to run. I started running. When I arrived at home, I finally got a chance to see what the judges were doing with my case. When I looked in my file the judges were falsifying my court records! There were different judges signing and changing dates on my court records. They were all in division 6.

I went to the library to study law. Through my study I found out that falsifying court records is a crime punishable in the USA, punishment generally according to stature. This was a time for me to pray and hear from the Lord. I prayed and the Lord gave me an answer. The Lord told me that I was leaving KC soon. I waited for Him to open the door. Isaiah 40:23 That bringeth the princes to nothing: he maketh the judges of the earth as vanity.

Chapter 8

I was listening to the radio one morning. There was this woman named Jean Coyle talking about a book she wrote named "Bye Bye Baby the Stealing of America's Children." Because Jean had written the book, I knew she had some experience in helping parents who have experienced such tragedy. She gave her phone number on the air to offer her help. When I called Jean she answered the phone, I explained to her my situation. She offered me a way out of KC. She set up a team of sisters to meet me at my sister Joy's house. However, we were not only just to meet there. I was told to go in the Taylor's house to take LaTosha and bring her with me. We made the plan and everybody agreed to the plan. Somehow I knew the

Taylor's were going to let me see LaTosha. Their reason for me not to have legal visitation was to hurt me and control me. Joy picked me up as planned. I was welcomed into the Taylor's house. Mr. Taylor was in the living room watching tv. Mrs. Taylor was in the kitchen talking to me. LaTosha was holding my hand real tight. Suddenly LaTosha yelled, "Run mom!" We began to run. She did not know there was a plan in place. God put it on her heart that we were going to get her out of there that day. Joy was waiting for us with the van door wide open. We jumped in and she took off. By the time she pulled off, we could see Mr. Taylor falling down in the driveway trying to catch us. The plan was in full effect. Joy arrived in front of her house and the sisters were there to meet us. We got out of Joy's van and got straight into their car. The next part of the plan was to get LaTosha and me to the greyhound bus station safely. We were headed to Rowlet, Texas where Jean lived.

They had friends that were policemen to check if any reports of kidnap were reported. There were no alerts so they took us to the greyhound bus station. They watched us leave. We arrived in Rowlet, Texas safely. Jean met us at the bus station. She took us to her house where she made us feel welcome. Jean looked at my court records. She said I was right. What the Taylors and the judges were doing is illegal Jean told me that the petition for me to accommodate a place for me and my child was unconstitutional I have the right to live where I desire because I was never proven unfit.. She also mentioned that she had seen some court papers to take away my son Isaiah. He was still living in KC with my mother. Although Jean was helping me with my case, she asked me to help her to work on some other cases. I met this guy named Raymond while working on the cases. I had to present him with some paper work. He was a very confident man. I gave him his information. He smiled at me then asked me to turn around. I smiled back and did like he asked. Later Roberta, Raymond's sister, exchanged phone numbers for Raymond and I. Roberta had been working with Jean and me on Raymond's case. Raymond and I start dating.

    I was blessed with a job at Sanger Harris Department Store. I worked in the Advertising Department as a data entry operator. It was the now Christmas Season and Sanger Harris had major advertising campaigns to launch. I was responsible for sending new fashions to New York, California, and Atlanta. My supervisor gave me the fashion ads and matched them up with the cities that they were to be mailed to. Turns out, I found something wrong with the ads she had matched up. I did not mail the ads. Instead, I went to my supervisor and talked to her about the way I thought the ads should go. She was so glad I didn't mail them like she told me. As a matter of fact, she said I saved Sanger Harris for their Christmas Campaign. We decided the way I had matched the ads were right. I sealed the envelopes and sent them to their destinations. I was happy about that, but I still had serious business to settle in my personal life. After learning from Jean that the court was trying to take Isaiah away from me, I had to come up with a plan. While I was contemplating going back to KC the Lord gave me a dream. I dreamt that I went to KC to get Isaiah and they took LaTosha from me. A few days later, I was talking to some friends about going back to KC to get Isaiah and they offered to keep LaTosha until I returned. I had to trust to them because God had already warned me in a dream. Obediently, I asked my friends would they keep LaTosha for seven days. They agreed. LaTosha also felt alright about staying. I made it a point to give them money to help out with expenses. With much expectation, I made my reservation on the greyhound for a round trip from Dallas to KC and back.

  When I arrived in KC I got Isaiah from my mom. Unfortunately, she had been in a car wreck and had broken her neck. I found out from her that Mrs. Taylor had been in a car accident too. Nevertheless to avoid trouble with the law I stayed away from the Taylors. Franklin escorted Isaiah and I to the bus station to make sure no one bothered us.

  When Isaiah and I arrived at Doris's house LaTosha was so happy to see me and her brother. We all were hugging and laughing and praising God. When I was reunited with my children, the Lord spoke to me and said you must go to California. Jerry, one the people I was staying with, started flirting with me. He was a married man. There was no way I was going to sleep with him. I had a lot respect for his wife. One day his cousin Bo came over to the house. Bo asked me did I want to go home with him. I said yes, he said ok pack your clothes and I will take you and the little ones home with me. I was happy that worked out because Jerry would not quit trying to get with me. I packed my bags, grabbed my children and I let Bo know that I was ready to go. Bo said go get into my car I'm coming. All of a sudden, Jerry comes running after me, I jumped in the car with my children and locked the door. When I looked up Bo and Jerry were fighting. I heard Bo say "I'm not gonna let you jump on this woman for nothing!" Jerry yelled, "we are cousins she ain't nothing to us." Bo beat him up and said, "no you are not going to touch her." I was happy to be at Bo and Mary's house. I knew that Jerry would not come over here to bother me anymore. While I was at Bo's house I told Bo I was in need of a job so he gave me the job advertisements. I saw a job I was qualified for. I called the job and I talked with a supervisor. She told me that the job position was hard to fill. She asked me had I one any numeric filing I replied "no, but there hasn't been a job yet that I was not able to do." She said "you are hired!" I said "without an application?" She said "yes. Report to the Southland Corporation in the morning at 8:00 am." I was so excited, she gave me more information about the job before our call ended. Bo and Mary were happy for me. Bo took me back and forth to work. My first day on the job, I learned to do the numeric filing well. Picking up my first check was exciting. I had to go to a place that I' had never been before. I had to go downtown Dallas, Tx. it was great. When I arrived at the suite I didn't hesitate to enter. There was somebody to greet me. They had been waiting for me. She said "are you Frances Roland?" I replied yes, then she introduced me to another young lady. She told her "this is the young lady they worked our numeric filing system, we hadn't been able to find anyone else to do it." She congratulated me and gave me my check she also thanked me for doing such a good job. Bo and Mary decided it was time for them to go back to Church.

Raymond and I were still in a relationship and I had become pregnant. He called me one day while I was working to say that he had something important to tell me. When I saw him, he said that he had an apartment for the children and I and that he desired for us live with him. He also said that he wanted to marry me. LaTosha yanked my arm and said "no mom." I looked in her face I remembered the Lord told me I had to go to California. I told Raymond I had to go because I had to reach California. He didn't want us to go and part of me didn't want to go either.

I was watching J. Swaggart's Ministry on television, and I got an idea. I called J. Swaggart Ministry and asked them if they could help me with my case. I let them know I had the court papers. I had one issue. They said that I was out of their jurisdiction. I asked them if I come there would they help me and they said yes. I left Dallas and went to Baton Rouge, LA. When I arrived at J.Swaggart's Ministry they said that they could not help me. I explained to them that I had already talked to them on the phone. I cried and asked them "so yall just misleading people for no good reason at all?" I was disappointed. Despite my disappointment, they did let me know of a family shelter where we could stay. I felt like Jonah and I knew that I had to get to California.

I asked if the staff at the family shelter could they buy me ticket to California. In the meantime, the shelter was in their own conspiracy. I went over Gladys house. she lived next door to the shelter. When Annette came over, she told me that she had heard the ladies in the office say that they had no intentions of helping me get to California. Annette put her hands in her pocket and handed me $200! She said "take your children and go to

California." I thanked Jesus and I thanked her for my surprise blessing. The Lord will make a way out of no way.

When I arrived at the greyhound bus station the Lord told me Los Angeles CA was my destination. I felt reassured that the Lord was with me. I was looking for a sign as to where to go in Los Angeles. A scripture was on my mind. Proverbs 3:5 Acknowledge God in all thy ways and He shall direct your paths. My first stop was the Los Angeles Church of God in Christ. I went in asked to talk to the Pastor. I showed him my file. He appointed Queen Esther and her husband to help us and give us a place to stay. They charged us $350 a month for a room. I was very uncomfortable there. Queen Esther kept talking bad about us on the phone. We went to bed early and I knew we weren't going to be staying there long. Later on that night her husband came beating at my bedroom door. He was yelling "Queen Esther dead!" I put my robe on and went into the living room. I asked him what happened. He said she had just finished talking on the phone with Sister Rutland, then suddenly the dogs start barking loudly. He went outside to check on them, and when he came back in Queen Esther was laid across the sofa dead. I consoled him and I let him know that he was in my prayers. He told me we could still stay but I turned down the offer.

My children and I were invited to live with Sister Julie and her family. They treated us like family. I helped her with her family and she helped me with mine. We were a blessing to each other. The Lord showed me when to move on. Which was the time it was closer for me to deliver.

I moved to Los Angeles Watts with Lynn and Eric. once again they treated us like family.

A Praying Mother

Lynn's mom is an Evangelist. Lynn introduced me to her brother Dexter. Dexter was a good friend. He was easy to talk to. I decided to tell him about my custody battle while I was washing dishes one night. I heard some noise and when I turned around he was crying. I simply asked him "why are you crying?" And he said "you are way up there, a leader like Jessie or somebody". I comforted him and said to him, "I been living for Jesus since I was a young girl, and He's the reason why I can stand and fight against the enemy. We all had a good time talking about the Lord. Lynn's sister came over and made homemade burritos for everybody." Dexter told me that he was going to church with me Sunday morning. He kept his word and I was surprised to see him stand up and give his life to Christ during the Altar call. I lived at Dexter's mom's house until I delivered.

    Lance Dion was born at the French Hospital in LA
    California to myself and Raymond

After Lance was born, we lived in Los Angeles about 3 months. I was arrested for kidnap of LaTosha. My Children were sent to a Children's home except for LaTosha. I found out later that Victor flew from KC and took her back with him. I was held in LA jail for those KC judges to come and state their case against me. The KC judges never showed up and I had been in jail for two weeks. A trustee in the jail came up to me and told me that the judges in KC fail to show up, so my mom was coming to pick me up. I was thanking and praising the Lord that I was getting ready to be released. I also thought about those crooked Judges in Kansas,. the fact that they had no evidence of kidnap. The protection of God was all around me , and the judges fell back. False accusations and the false imprisonment;. I really should have pressed charges against the judges for deformation of character and mental anguish. I was happy to be free and I decided to focus on being awarded custody of my children than to bring allegations against the judges. My mom came to the jail to pick me up. She had my sons with her. She had already had them release from the Children's home. When I walked out my sisters and my mom were acting out hear no evil, see no evil, and speak no evil. I laughed. I was happy to see them. I had saved some money so we all went shopping in downtown LA and I bought them all new clothes. We were all anticipating a long ride back to KC.

December of 1986 County of Los Angeles Department of Children services held court for the custody of Lance and Isaiah. The Judge said to me "It was wrong what they did to you in KC about LaTosha. I now have jurisdiction in this custody matter. If you go through therapy and take a parenting class, give me something to stand on, I'll give you custody of your sons and I'll make sure you see LaTosha. I replied "yes Sir." My mom was there. She was given temporary custody of my two sons. Mom and I enjoyed the airplane flight back to KC. The plan for me to go through therapy and parenting classes was just not happening at this time. Mom and I were not getting along. Living there with her, in her house, with my sons was not easy.

Chapter 9

One afternoon, Tudy and I were shopping at the Food Arena grocery. There I met Traci. He came up to me and asked me if I were married. I answered no. my answer made him smile. He asked me for my name and number. I gave him the information that he asked for and he said "I'm sure going to call you." Traci kept his word. We start talking and he began to visit me at my mother's house. Traci did not like my mother's house. He talked about taking me to Chicago one day.

At that time, I was talking to my brother Algadean. He had his own house in Missouri. He gave me permission to come live with him. I accepted the offer and moved out of my mom's house. No matter what I did I still kept my children in my thoughts, in my heart and in my prayers. Algadean's wife, Tammy, was a supervisor for RL Polk's Publishing Co. She mentioned to me that they were hiring at this time. She also said that I should apply for a job there. January of 1987 I was hired as a claims examiner for Polk Publishing Co. Meanwhile, Traci was working construction.

Traci asked me to meet him at Crown Center. I agreed and showed up. When I saw him bearing presents. I went up to him. He said, "Come with me." I followed him. We went to the entertainment part of the hotel where there was a pianist playing soft music. It was there that he proposed to me one knee. He bought me this yellow fitted long flared jacket with a matching skirt. He also brought me a pair of white lace pumps. The ring was so pretty. Two months later, March 1, 1987 Traci and I were married. We were married at Church by Bishop Warren. I was wearing a white lace dress, with my white lace pumps, and white lace gloves. Traci wore a suit. It was a private wedding. Anyone could see that I was moving too fast.

Frances Lang

A Praying Mother

Chapter 10

Our move to Chicago had come to pass. Traci told me that all the land was flat in Chicago. The land there had no hills. It was true. Traci found a job while I enrolled in First Business Word-processing School. The school was located downtown Chicago. We lived in an apartment on 50th and Kenmore. We were on the North Side.

As time passed I began to think about my children. One day I was watching the Oprah Show. They announced on the show that they were looking for parents who had custody battles where the courts are not displaying the current status. Once again, I saw an opportunity to get somebody to look at the court records in my possession and help me with my case. They displayed a phone number for Oprah. I called the number. When my call was answered I was asked me to explain why I should be on Oprah's Show. I explained my case. He said, "Yes, you qualify to be on the show." I said, "Yay!" The number he gave me was 77. He also gave me instructions to wear light clothing and be at the Oprah Studio early.

We arrived at the Oprah Studio early, as we were advised. I was asked several questions about my case. I made it to the second stage of screening, but Oprah did not choose to present my case on television. I was not mad. Maybe disappointed plus Oprah shook my hand when the session was over. When Traci and I got home all we could say was that we're trying. Things still seemed hopeless. I still kept faith in GOD. The Bible says in Mark 9:23

Jesus said unto him, "If thou can believe, all things are possible to him that believeth."

I received the news that I was expecting a child. Being pregnant interfered with my education. I had to take a leave of absence from First Business a month before my delivery. Daniel was born during the Christmas Season. He was born the day after Thanksgiving. Soon after Daniels birth, during my postpartum, I began missing my children and desiring to be with them. As a mother I felt hurt and betrayed not knowing when I was ever going to hold or see my children again. I was having a tough time dealing with everything. I boiled a pot of hot water to sterilize some scissors and I cut a little piece of the foreskin from Daniel's genital area.. Traci took Daniel to the doctor. There was no damage done but he knew I needed help with my children. He called my family in KC and they made arrangements for me to come back to KC.

Chapter 11

When I arrived at my mom's house I felt so much better. I was able to see Lance and Isaiah. Oh how I missed them. I was glad to be back with them. I was also thinking about Daniel. I was so glad that he was not harmed in anyway. Thanks to the Lord. I still had a lot to deal with.

Daniel was in Chicago with Traci. Lance and Isaiah were still in my mom's custody, under the jurisdiction of LA California, and LaTosha was with her grandmother also in KC. Mr. Taylor died when we were in California. Unfortunately, Traci start threatening me about taking custody of Daniel. I know I've made some mistakes but I thought after all I had been through that he would have been more understanding. I went in my bedroom, closed the door and kneeled down on my knees to pray. "Dear Lord I love you very much, and I need you right now. I know you have all power in Heaven and Earth in your hands. I believe there's nothing to hard or impossible for you. Please reunite my children and I together. I'm thanking you in advance. Thank you, precious sweet Lord Jesus for the restoration of my children. In the name of Jesus I pray, amen." I later had a talk with my mom. She told me that the case in California was still open. She said that she still had temporary custody through Los Angles court. The judge was still waiting for me to complete the therapy and parenting classes. Wow! This was a miracle. It took me about 2 years before I was able to do what the judge asked of me. My mom gave me the name of my case worker. Her name is Ms. Arnold Mom also gave me the phone number to reach her in California. I hurried to call Ms. Arnold She was glad to hear from me. I reassured her I was ready to comply with the Judge's order to take the classes in order for me to have the custody of my children. She said, "Great!" I told her about being married and what I did to my son. She encouraged me and said, "It will all be alright." Ms. Arnold said not to worry about what Traci is doing or going to do. "You need to get enrolled in the classes, then call me and give me the information concerning them." She said if I had any problems to call and let her know.

Although my mom's house was talked about by some people, I Knew what I had to do to get my mom's house in order to eliminate negative feedback when California Awards me custody of my children. I also desired to be comfortable with my children there. I was grateful that my mom took care of my children. She is a blessing to me.

I enrolled in a program at Wyandotte Mental Health Center. My Counselor/Therapist was Sylvia I began the counseling then I enrolled in a parenting class. Meanwhile, I had to go court in Chicago concerning Daniel. My attorney Mr. Trainor explained to the judge that I was in counseling. When I arrived back in KC, I was having a tough time in counseling dealing with the Taylor's. They had all these what and why's questions about what happened to Daniel in Chicago. I felt like my life was not my own. My personal life was on trial and being invaded. I did learn some strategies for coping with stress.

Finally, I completed counseling successfully! Praise God. Next, I started my parenting class. The parenting class was much better and very interesting. I enjoyed the class especially the different approaches to parenting. I completed the parenting class successfully. Thank you, Sweet Lord Jesus. The program took about a year to complete. The County of Los Angeles Department Children Services, Awarded I, (Frances Roland) custody of the minor Franklin (Isaiah) (DOB8/6/84) and Lance (DOB8/19/86 Roland on August 4, 1989. 1Corinthians 15:57. Thanks be to God, which giveth us the victory through our Lord Jesus Christ.

According to Chicago court, it was also time for me to be reunited with Daniel. Traci welcomed us all home. Now was the time for me to enjoy being restored to my three sons while living in Chicago. I couldn't stop thinking about LaTosha.

Therefore, I came up with a plan to get all my family back to KC so that we could be closer to LaTosha. They were allowing me to see LaTosha without legal visitation rights. I convinced Traci to move back to KC and we did.

Frances Lang

Chapter 12

At that time, Traci had rented us an apartment at Chesapeake Estates in Johnson County, KS. I remember listening to the radio on a gospel station one day, and I heard them announce that Rerun was coming to a Church in Johnson County. I really wanted to attend that service. I memorized the phone number to the Church. I called them to ask if they could arrange for me to have transportation to the special event. They said yes. The arrangement for me to have transportation was made. I was asked for my address and phone number. They returned my phone call to give me information about the family that was going to pick us up. They told me their name and the time and the color and make of their car. On the day of the blessed event, the blessed couple showed up on time to pick us up.

They took us to Church and sat with us. When we arrived at the church Rerun was just beginning to speak. He talked about his drug addiction to cocaine. He had a $1000 a day habit. He mentioned the fact that lots of people in Hollywood are on drugs. Everything was different for him now. He had given his life to Jesus. The Lord had delivered him from his cocaine habit. Rerun asked if anyone in the congregation use to dance. If so, raise your hand. I raised my hand. The shocking part was, he asked everyone that raised their hand to come up front. I was still a little shy, believe it or not. I had my three sons with me but our friends offered to keep them. Slowly, I went up front to the Altar where was standing. He said "you all know ya'll would dance in the world, so come on and dance for Jesus." He said, "We're going to play some music and when the music starts dance.

The music started I began to dance like, the Lockers, Rerun former dance group. He looked at me pointed and smiled. He did some Lockers too.

He closed with a special tribute to the Lord. In which, he did the robot. It was such a blessing for me to see Rerun giving glory to God and living his life for Jesus. I see Rerun now on the show What's Happening!! That show still premiers on TV one channel and other channels. I really enjoyed dancing for the Lord with him. When I was younger I danced with the Junior Lockers. I never could imagine that I would dance with a real Locker!

While living in Johnson County, Traci was a really being mean to our children. I could not stand the way he treated them. I didn't fight for them, just to have somebody mistreat them. I left Traci. I did not know at the time, I was pregnant. I called my attorney Mr. Trainor in Chicago and asked him about the custody of Daniel. First, he congratulated me on Being Awarded custody of Isaiah and Lance. Mr.Trainor said, "When you get your divorce in KC you will get custody of Daniel as well."

Traci was following me around. He found out where I lived. Traci snatched Daniel out of my yard one day. he was missing for three days. I'm not sure what happened during the time. Traci's friend brought Daniel Back. I filed for a divorce and I was issued a restraining order against Traci. Because I was pregnant, I had to wait before the divorce was final. I gave birth to Lina during the Christmas Season. December 11, 1990. She was named after my favorite grandmother (Dear) Lina Roland. My grandmother was still living. I had to fight for Lina to have the Roland last name. The nurses came in to fill out the birth certificate. I told them her last name is to be Roland. They asked me how that could be when the mom and dad have a different last name. I told them, "I had filed for a divorce. Roland is my maiden name". I showed them my restraining order because I didn't want Traci coming to the hospital. I needed to show them some evidence. They told me to wait so they could see if it were legal. The nurses came back and said yes since Roland is your maiden name.

February 21, 1991 Traci and I were divorced. I was granted custody of Daniel and Lina. My maiden name was restored. When Lina was born, I went to visit my grandmother (Lina). By this time in her life, she was sick and in bed. I entered into her room. She was not responded to little Lina and I. I told her, "I'll Be back we love you." I went back about a week later. As I entered Dear's room with little Lina, she raised up and smiled at me. I said "Dear, here's little Lina name after you." she started crying. "Oh! Frances that so sweet, she's a blessing." Though my grandma might have been sick in her body, her mind was still sharp.

June 29. 1991 My grandmother went to be with the Lord. I know I had a praying grandmother. She lived to see all my children restored back to me except for LaTosha. The date on my custody papers from County of LA Department of Children's Services. Is March 14,1990. That's my grandmother Lina and my grandpa Dewitt's birthday.

Chapter 13

The Lord maketh the Judges of the earth as vanity.
Isaiah 40:23.

My children would cry because they missed LaTosha. It wasn't all at the same time, but each one of them had their moments. We knew that things would be turning around for us real soon when it came to visitation rights to LaTosha.

In the meantime, my children were growing up. They were being raised in the Church. I start teaching them to dance for the Lord. They began to perform in Christmas Programs. We decide to use our gifts for the Lord. We rehearsed at home. The first thing we would do is pray and ask the Lord what he would have us to do and the song. After we are given the song then we start rehearsals. We moved the furniture around so that we can have the space to dance. There is no company, no television or any distractions. We focus strictly on our dance. The choreography comes first, then we take the rest of the time for rehearsals.

The first Christmas Program they performed in was at New Beginnings Church. They danced to the Jackson 5 Christmas song "Up on the housetop". They also had parts in the Christmas play. Lina was a sheep in the play. she didn't participate in the dance. I did a praise dance in the program to the song "What shall I render?" I also performed mime. I have this Christmas program on DVD. Our next performance was December of 1997 in The Christmas Program "Jesus is the reason for the season". They all danced to 'Candy Rain". I did a praise dance to "Stand up for right" by O'landa Draper. We had lots of fun at Church Margret and Cocoa, and Tawana, and KeKe performed "Behold the Lamb" That performance was Amazing. Brother John, the Storyteller, he had a rap about Christmas that made me appreciate the art. The Sounds of Glory Choir sang to the Glory of God. The Christmas Program was surely awesome. To God be the glory.

For the year of 1998, LaTosha and I performed in the Christmas Program "A King is born" We did a praise dance to God's Grace "by Trinity 5:7. The Maudella Roland Jesus Steppers from the Pleasant Green Baptist Church performed also.

Victory Temple Presents another Christmas Program "Celebrate Jesus for the Lord is coming!' LaTosha, Lina and I did a praise dance, we performed to the song 'Praising on my mind" by Dawkins and Dawkins. Mechanical Man performed to the song

"Miracle Worker". I was impressed. They really looked like mechanical men (robots). Every year we had a Christmas Program. We had apples, and candy sacks for all the Children. We had the Children's Choir for the children and we always had a Christmas play. We have posters and DVD's of Christmas Programs and other Church Programs. I love to be a part of what's going on at Church, especially at Christmas.

I love gospel music and oldie but goody love songs. My favorite songs is Jesus Christ is the way" by Walter Hawkins. You thought I was worth saving by Anthony Brown. I still praise dance for the Lord at different Churches that host programs for any particular reason. I recently performed "We shall behold Him" by Vickie Winans. Psalm 30:11 Thou hast turned my mourning into dancing!

A Praying Mother

LaTosha was giving Jesus her best while she was living with the Taylors. She didn't let being separated from me stop her. She had learned a poem about Dr. Martin Luther King Jr. and she was invited to different Churches and Schools to recite it. She won several awards and trophies from School. She won trophies for the highest test scores for the CTBS test and she won one trophy for student of the year. I was proud of her accomplishments. She excelled in school and received a letter to attend Sumner Academy. Sumner Academy is a School of Arts and Science. Sumner is a college preparatory school for more advanced students.

As for the Taylors, Mr. Taylor died while we were in California. Mrs. Taylor had no help because Victor was still on crack. He had lost his job at Santa Fe. He lost his car and everything. Mrs. Taylor became friends with me. She let me see LaTosha as much as I desired to. She even brought LaTosha over to my house. She came over on Christmas and Easter and celebrated the holidays and birthdays with all of us. She loved my sweet potato pie. I made her one every holiday especially the Christmas Season. LaTosha was growing up and the Lord had blessed us with a mother-daughter bond that could not be broken. At graduation time, she was sure that she desired to live with me and her brothers and sister as opposed to staying alone with her grandmother. LaTosha knew that her grandmother had money, but she was not going to let that keep her there. I attended her graduation but Victor did not. He was in town. Supposedly instead of coming to her graduation, he ran off with some friends to get high, so we been told. He did not come to

LaTosha's graduation. LaTosha graduated from Sumner Academy with honors.

After LaTosha graduated, she came home driving a brand new red neon. I remember having to stand up to Mrs. Taylor. She didn't want LaTosha to learn how to drive at school. I was able to convince her to let LaTosha take drivers Ed. When LaTosha came home. It was one of the happiest moments of my life. I was full of joy with tears streaming down my face as we began to laugh as we embraced. I began to thank Jesus loudly. The rest of my children cae running out the house to welcome her home. I could hardly believe it. Oh how I prayed and thanked

God for this day to come. After all these years she came home to be with her family. When I was in jail he made the judges fall back. when LaTosha made the decision to come home Jesus shut the judges and the Taylors down.. In spite of all I went thru in the physical and the mental I had to trust God in the spiritual realm . I won custody of all my children over eighteen years period of time. I don't know what I do if the Lord wasn't on my side. Psalm 124:2,3 If it had not been the Lord who was on our side , when men rose up against us: Then they would have swallowed us up quick.

We all told LaTosha that we loved her. We were all one big happy family. We had a dinner for LaTosha to welcome her home. We served ham, dressing, yams, green beans, and macaroni with cheese. She love strawberries. I made sure she had them.

LaTosha still have a relationship with her grandma Taylor. Sometimes God takes years to answer our prayers. But what I love about God is He will answer. 11Thessalonians 3:3-4 But the Lord is faithful who shall stablish you and keep you from evil

A Praying Mother

Chapter 14

This is what's happening now. Unfortunately, Mrs. Taylor went to be with the Lord. However Victor is still not a part of LaTosha's life. He's still doesn't call her, or come to see her. She doesn't even know where he lives. After all that trouble he raised about LaTosha, he is not interested in having anything to do with her. Traci he's sort of the same way. he doesn't call his children, nor does he respond to them calling him, and he lives in KC. Franklin finally stepped after realizing whtat was right.. He began to pay child support. he also began to visit with Isaiah and invite him to his house. He also gave him money. Franklin died recently of cancer. Raymond has a relationship with Lance. Lance was inspired by me to find Raymond on the internet and he was successful. Thanks to God.

As for my children. All my children graduated from school. They all furthered their education. LaTosha has a career as a claims technician for an insurance company. she has a son named Cameron. Isaiah has a trade in carpentry, but he specializes in custom cabinetry and architectural millwork. Lance is the founder and CEO of a professional home health care agency. Lance has two children Luke Skyelar and Luzila Skye. Daniel is the designer of his own clothing line (certified A+). He also has a partnership with a restaurant where he has his own item on the menu "Danny's cinnamon sweet hot wings. He has two children, Rhyan and Astro. Lina has a career in cosmetology, she has a son named Levi. As for me, I went to college and received my Child Development Associate. I am qualified to work as an Assistant Pre-School Teacher. By God's grace and mercy. He blessed

Raymond and I to be reunited after 30 yrs., and we are blessed and glad to be back in each other's arms again. We have been happily married for five years and counting now. All my children are very close we talk on a regular basis. We spend Easter and Christmas together. My children and my grandchildren love to sit around and watch the Christmas Programs on DVD. Skye my granddaughter also has a DVD where she is acting in a Christmas Program. During the holidays I don't have to do much of the cooking anymore. Daniel is a chef. He can really cook. I taught him some of what he knows, but now he's teaching me. The holidays are much easier for me. I have more time to relax. To God be the Glory for the things he has done.

     Romans 8:28 and we know that all things work together for good to them that love God to them who are the called according to His purpose. It may seem like I did things all alone but I did not.

The Lord blessed me with my Aunt Carol. She was always praying with me and for me. My Aunt Earline and Uncle Ronnie, Aunt Norma also prayed for our family/. Mother Lena was another one that prayed for my family. Nevertheless the Lord Jesus Christ Himself was with me all the time. The Lord said: "I will never leave thee or forsake thee." Hebrews 13:

 My mom and I have a better relationship. She's there for me, especially when I need her. She has accepted Jesus Christ in her life and she attends church. She has been married 43 years.

    For all the promises of God in Him are yea, and in Him Amen, unto the glory of God by us,I have kept the faith. Thus I'll be watching and waiting for the promise of the Lord Jesus to return. My high highest dream. 1Thessalonians 4:16 For the Lord Himself, shall descend from Heaven with a shout with the voice of the Archangel, and with the trump of God: and the dead in Christ shall rise first: Then we which are alive and remain shall be caught up together with them in the clouds, to meet the Lord in the air and so shall we ever be with the Lord. Amen

To God Be The Glory

www.ingramcontent.com/pod-product-compliance
Lightning Source LLC
Chambersburg PA
CBHW052124110526
44592CB00013B/1738